SIDE BY SIDE

English
Through
Guided Conversations
1B

Steven J. Molinsky

Bill Bliss

Illustrated by

Richard E. Hill

Prentice-Hall Inc., Englewood Cliffs, New Jersey 07632

Library of Congress Cataloging in Publication Data

MOLINSKY, STEVEN J.
   Side by Side

   Includes indexes.
     1. English language—Conversation and phrase books.
2. English language—Text books for foreign speakers.
I. Bliss, Bill. II. Title.
PE1131.M58 1983   428.3'4   82-20425
ISBN 0-13-809723-2 (Book 1B)

Printed in the United States of America

15   14   13   12   11

Editorial/production supervisor: Penelope Linskey
Art/camera copy supervisor: Diane Heckler-Koromhas
Cover design by Suzanne Behnke
Manufacturing buyer: Harry P. Baisley

0-13-809723-2

PRENTICE-HALL INTERNATIONAL, INC., *London*
PRENTICE-HALL OF AUSTRALIA PTY. LIMITED, *Sydney*
EDITORA PRENTICE-HALL DO BRASIL, LTDA., *Rio de Janeiro*
PRENTICE-HALL OF CANADA, LTD., *Toronto*
PRENTICE-HALL OF INDIA PRIVATE LIMITED, *New Delhi*
PRENTICE-HALL OF JAPAN, INC., *Tokyo*
PRENTICE-HALL OF SOUTHEAST ASIA PTE. LTD., *Singapore*
WHITEHALL BOOKS LIMITED, WELLINGTON, *New Zealand*

Contents

BOOK 1A

Contents

BOOK **1B**

Side by Side is a conversational grammar book.

We do not seek to describe the language, or prescribe its rules. Rather, we aim to help students learn to *use* the language grammatically, through practice with meaningful conversational exchanges.

This book is intended for adult and young-adult learners of English. It is designed to provide the beginning student with the basic foundation of English grammar, through a carefully sequenced progression of conversational exercises and activities. Teachers of nonbeginning students will also find these materials to be effective as a rapid, concise review of basic structures of the language.

WHY A CONVERSATIONAL GRAMMAR BOOK?

Grammar is usually isolated and drilled through a variety of traditional structural exercises such as repetition, substitution, and transformation drills. These exercises effectively highlight particular grammatical structures . . . but they are usually presented as a string of single sentences, not related to each other in any unifying, relevant context.

Traditional dialogues, on the other hand, may do a fine job of providing examples of real speech, but they don't usually offer sufficient practice with the structures being taught. Teachers and students are often frustrated by the lack of a clear grammatical focus in these meaningful contexts. And besides that, it's hard to figure out what to *do* with a dialogue after you've read it, memorized it, or talked about it.

In this book we have attempted to combine the best features of traditional grammatical drills and contextually rich dialogues. We aim to actively engage our students in meaningful conversational exchanges within carefully structured grammatical frameworks. And we encourage our students to then break away from the textbook and *use* these frameworks to create conversations *on their own*.

While we have designed this text for the beginning student, we are also concerned about the nonbeginner. Although this student has made progress in understanding and using the language, he or she often needs more practice with the basics, the "nuts and bolts" of elementary English grammar.

(Intermediate-level teachers often tell us that even though their students are doing beautifully with the present perfect tense, they still have trouble with such "early" structures as the third-person singular -*s* or the difference between the simple present and present continuous tenses.)

This book offers nonbeginners the opportunity to use their richer vocabularies in open-ended conversational exercises which focus on the basic grammatical structures of the language.

AN OVERVIEW

GRAMMATICAL PARADIGMS

Each lesson in the book covers one or more specific grammatical . structures. A new structure appears first in the form of a grammatical paradigm, a simple schema of the structure.

These paradigms are meant to be a reference point for students as they proceed through the lesson's conversational activities. While these paradigms highlight the structures being taught, we don't intend them to be goals in themselves.

We don't want our students simply to parrot back these rules: we want them to engage in conversations that show they can *use* them correctly.

GUIDED CONVERSATIONS

Guided conversations are the dialogues and the question and answer exchanges which are the primary learning devices in this book. Students are presented with a model conversation that highlights a specific aspect of the grammar. In the exercises that follow the model, students pair up and work "Side by Side," placing new content into the given conversational framework.

How to Introduce Guided Conversations

There are many alternative ways to introduce these conversations. We don't want to dictate any particular method. Rather, we encourage you to develop strategies that are compatible with your own teaching style, the specific needs of your students, and the particular grammar and content of the lesson at hand.

Some teachers will want books closed at this stage, so their students will have a chance to listen to the model before seeing it in print.

Other teachers will want students to have their books open for the model conversation or see it written on the blackboard. The teacher may read or act out the conversation while students follow along, or may read through the model with another student, or may have two students present the model to the class.

Whether books are open or closed, students should have ample opportunity to understand and practice the model before attempting the exercises that follow it.

How to Use Guided Conversations

In these conversational exercises, we are asking our students to place new content into the grammatical and contextual framework of the model. The numbered exercises provide the student with new information which is "plugged into" the framework of the model conversation. Sometimes this framework actually appears as a "skeletal dialogue" in the text. Other times the student simply inserts the new information into the model that has just been practiced. (Teachers who have written the model conversation on the blackboard can create the skeletal dialogue by erasing the words that are replaced in the exercises.)

The teacher's key function is to pair up students for "Side by Side" conversational practice, and then to serve as a resource to the class, for help with the structure, new vocabulary, and pronunciation.

"Side by Side" practice can take many forms. Most teachers prefer to call on two students at a time to present a conversation to the class. Other teachers have all their students pair up and practice the conversations with a partner. Or small groups of students might work together, pairing up within these groups and presenting the conversations to others in the group.

This paired practice helps teachers address the varying levels of ability of their students. Some teachers like to pair stronger students with weaker ones. The slower student clearly gains through this pairing, while the more advanced student also strengthens his or her abilities by lending assistance to the speaking partner.

Other teachers will want to pair up or group students of *similar* levels of ability. In this arrangement, the teacher can devote greater attention to students who need it, while giving more capable students the chance to learn from and assist each other.

While these exercises are intended for practice in conversation, teachers also find them useful as *writing* drills which reinforce oral practice and enable students to study more carefully the grammar highlighted in these conversations.

Once again, we encourage you to develop strategies that are most appropriate for your class.

The "Life Cycle" of a Guided Conversation

It might be helpful to define the different stages in the "life cycle" of a guided conversation.

1. *The Presentation Stage*
   The model conversation is introduced and practiced by the class.

2. *The Rehearsal Stage*
   Immediately after practicing the model, students do the conversational exercises that follow. For homework, they practice these conversations, and perhaps write out a few. Some lessons also ask students to create their own original conversations based on the model.

3. *The Performance Stage*
   The next day students do the conversational exercises in class, preferably with their textbooks and notebooks closed. Students shouldn't have to memorize these conversations. They will most likely remember them after sufficient practice in class and at home.

4. *The Incorporation Stage*
   The class reviews the conversation or pieces of the conversation in the days that follow. With repetition and time, the guided conversation "dissolves" and its components are incorporated into the student's active language.

ON YOUR OWN

An important component of each lesson is the "On Your Own" activity. These student-centered exercises reinforce the grammatical structures of the lesson while breaking away from the text and allowing students to contribute content of their own.

These activities take various forms: role-plays, interviews, extended guided conversations, and questions about the student's real world.

In these exercises, we ask students to bring to the classroom new content, based on their interests, their backgrounds, and the farthest reaches of their imaginations.

We recommend that the teacher read through these activities in class and assign them as homework for presentation the next day. In this way, students will automatically review the previous day's grammar while contributing new and inventive content of their own.

"On Your Own" activities are meant for simultaneous grammar reinforcement and vocabulary building. Beginning students will tend to recycle previous textbook vocabulary into these activities. While this repetition is clearly useful, beginners should also be encouraged to use other words which are familiar to them but are not in the text. *All* students should be encouraged to use a dictionary in completing the "On Your Own" activities. In this way, they will not only use the words they know, but the words they would *like* to know in order to really bring their interests, backgrounds, and imaginations into the classroom.

As a result, students will be teaching each other new vocabulary and also sharing a bit of their lives with others in the class.

CLASSROOM DRAMAS

"Classroom Dramas" are the full-page comic strip dialogues that appear every once in a while throughout the text. The goal of these dialogues is to tackle a specific grammatical structure and give students the opportunity to rehearse this structure in a short, playful classroom conversation.

Some teachers will simply want to read through these dramas with their students. Others might want to act them out, using students in the class as the characters.

Students enjoy memorizing these dramas and using them frequently throughout the course. In fact, they often break into these conversations spontaneously, without any prompting from the teacher. (Our students, for example, like to impress visitors to the class by confidently performing these dramas as though they were really happening for the first time.)

In conclusion, we have attempted to make the study of English grammar a lively and relevant experience for our students. While we hope that we have conveyed to you the substance of our textbook, we also hope that we have conveyed the spirit: that learning the grammar can be conversational . . . student-centered . . . and fun.

Steven J. Molinsky
Bill Bliss

18

Like to

Review of Tenses:
 Simple Present
 Simple Past
 Future: Going to
Indirect Object Pronouns

Read and practice.

A. Are you going to cook spaghetti this week?

B. No, I'm not.
I cooked spaghetti LAST week,* and I don't like to cook spaghetti very often.

*You can also say:

yesterday morning, afternoon, evening
last night

last week, weekend, month, year
last Sunday, Monday, . . . Saturday
last spring, summer, fall (autumn), winter
last January, February, . . . December

1. Are you going to study English this weekend?

2. Are you going to watch TV tonight?

3. Are you going to drink coffee this morning?

4. Is Robert going to buy new clothes this year?

5. Are you going to have dessert this evening?

6. Is Tommy going to play baseball this Saturday?

7. Is Mr. Peterson going to plant flowers this spring?

8. Is Mrs. Johnson going to clean her apartment this week?

9. Are you going to go skiing this February?

10. Is Linda going to travel to Canada this August?

11. Are Mr. and Mrs. Smith going to London this summer?

12. Are you and your friends going to Miami this winter?

> I'm going to give my wife a present.
> I'm going to give   her   a present.

Read and practice.

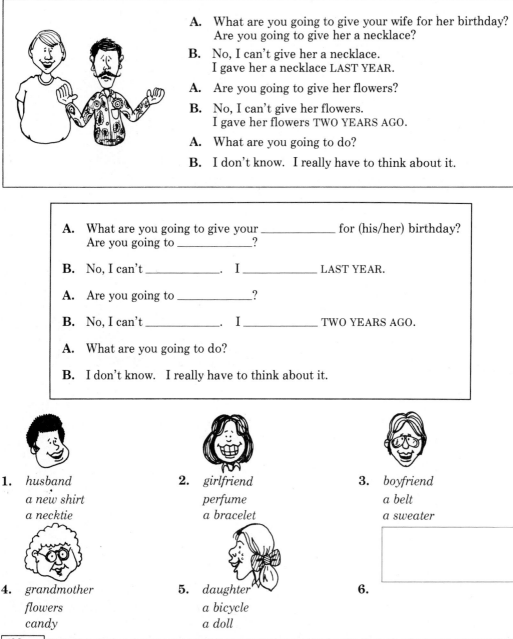

A. What are you going to give your wife for her birthday?
Are you going to give her a necklace?

B. No, I can't give her a necklace.
I gave her a necklace LAST YEAR.

A. Are you going to give her flowers?

B. No, I can't give her flowers.
I gave her flowers TWO YEARS AGO.

A. What are you going to do?

B. I don't know. I really have to think about it.

A. What are you going to give your _____ for (his/her) birthday?
Are you going to _____?

B. No, I can't _____. I _____ LAST YEAR.

A. Are you going to _____?

B. No, I can't _____. I _____ TWO YEARS AGO.

A. What are you going to do?

B. I don't know. I really have to think about it.

---

1. *husband*
a new shirt
a necktie

2. *girlfriend*
perfume
a bracelet

3. *boyfriend*
a belt
a sweater

4. *grandmother*
flowers
candy

5. *daughter*
a bicycle
a doll

6.

HARRY! I'M REALLY UPSET!

Read and practice.

Do you know what day this was?
It was my birthday, Harry. And you forgot again.
You didn't send me flowers.
You didn't give me candy.
You didn't buy me a present.
And you didn't even wish me "Happy Birthday."

Happy Birthday, Gladys!

I love you, Harry!

Why Was She Upset With Harry THIS Time?

1. He didn't _____ flowers.
2. _____ candy.
3. _____ a present.
4. _____ "Happy Birthday."

ON YOUR OWN

When is your birthday?
My birthday is _____.*

Tell the class about your last birthday.

What did you do?
Did you receive any presents?
What did you get?
Did your family or friends do
   anything special for you?
What did they do?

*See page xvi for how to read a date. You can
 say, for example, January 23rd (twenty-third),
 November 16th (sixteenth), June 9th (ninth).

19

Count/Non-Count Nouns

WHAT'S IN HENRY'S KITCHEN?

Count Nouns	Non-Count Nouns
tomatoes	cheese
eggs	milk
bananas	ice cream
apples	bread

Add foods from YOUR kitchen.

1. Let's make a salad for dinner!
   Sorry _____ lettuce.

2. Let's make an omelette for breakfast!
   Sorry _____ eggs.

3. Let's make some fresh lemonade!
   Sorry _____ lemons.

4. Let's bake a cake for dessert!
   Sorry _____ flour.

5. Let's make pizza for lunch!
   Sorry _____ cheese.

6. Let's make some fresh orange juice for breakfast!
   Sorry _____ oranges.

7. Let's make chicken and rice for dinner!
   Sorry _____ chicken.

8. Let's have french fries with our hamburgers!
   Sorry _____ potatoes.

9. Let's _____!
   Sorry _____.

much	many
how much?	how many?
too much	too many
so much that	so many that

A. You look terrible! What's the matter?

B. I drank TOO MUCH milk this morning.

A. HOW MUCH milk did you drink?

B. I drank SO MUCH milk that I'm never going to drink milk again!

A. You look terrible! What's the matter?

B. I ate TOO MANY cookies last night.

A. HOW MANY cookies did you eat?

B. I ate SO MANY cookies that I'm never going to eat a cookie again!

1. *drink . . . coffee*

2. *eat . . . tomatoes*

3. *buy . . . lettuce*

4. *smoke . . . cigarettes*

5. *wash . . . dishes*

6. *drink . . . wine*

7. *write . . . letters*

8. *have . . . ice cream*

9. *sing . . . songs*

10. *read . . . books*

11. *eat . . . cheese*

12. _____

a little	a few
coffee	apples
ice cream	eggs
butter	oranges

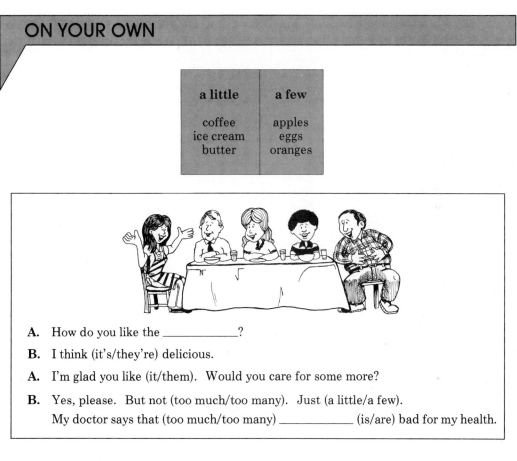

A. How do you like the _____?

B. I think (it's/they're) delicious.

A. I'm glad you like (it/them). Would you care for some more?

B. Yes, please. But not (too much/too many). Just (a little/a few).
My doctor says that (too much/too many) _____ (is/are) bad for my health.

Try this conversation with other students in your class, using these foods and others.

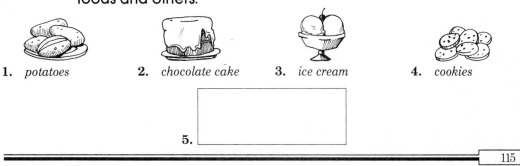

1. *potatoes* **2.** *chocolate cake* **3.** *ice cream* **4.** *cookies*

5.

Partitives
Count/Non-Count Nouns
Imperatives

My Shopping List

- a can of beans
- a jar of jam
- a bottle of soda
- a box of cereal
- a bag of flour
- a loaf of white bread
- 2 loaves of whole wheat bread
- a bunch of bananas
- 2 bunches of carrots
- a head of lettuce
- a lb.* of butter
- ½ lb.* of cheese

a quart of milk
a pack of cigarettes
a dozen eggs

*a lb. = a pound; ½ lb. = a half pound, or half a pound.

What did YOU buy the last time you went shopping?

A. I'm going to the supermarket. Can I get anything for you?

B. Yes, I need some **bread.**

A. How many **loaves of bread** do you need?

B. Just one **loaf,** please.

1. *cereal*

2. *marmalade*

3. *soda*

4. *bananas*

5. *vegetable soup*

6. *whole wheat bread*

7. *flour*

8.

A. How much does **a head of lettuce** cost?

B. **A head of lettuce** costs **ninety-five cents** (95¢).*

A. **NINETY-FIVE CENTS?!** That's a lot of money!

B. You're right.
Lettuce is very expensive this week.

*25¢ = twenty-five cents
50¢ = fifty cents

    etc.

A. How much does **a pound of apples** cost?

B. **A pound of apples** costs **a dollar twenty-five** ($1.25). †

A. **A DOLLAR TWENTY-FIVE?!** That's a lot of money!

B. You're right.
Apples are very expensive this week.

†$1.00 = a dollar
 $1.50 = a dollar fifty
 $2.25 = two twenty-five
 $4.50 = four fifty

    etc.

1. *butter*

2. *carrots*

3. *milk*

4. *onions*

5. *Swiss cheese*

6. *bananas*

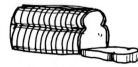

7. *white bread*

8. *oranges*

9.

AT THE RESTAURANT

A. What would you like **for dessert?**

B. I can't decide. What do you recommend?

A. I recommend our **chocolate ice cream.** Everybody says **it's** delicious.*

B. O.K. Please give me **a dish of chocolate ice cream.**

A. What would you like **for breakfast**?

B. I can't decide. What do you recommend?

A. I recommend our **scrambled eggs.** Everybody says **they're** out of this world.*

B. O.K. Please give me **an order of scrambled eggs.**

*Instead of delicious, you can also say:

fantastic
wonderful
magnificent
excellent
out of this world

What would you like . . .

1. . . . for dessert?
(a piece of) apple pie

2. . . . for lunch?
(a bowl of) chicken soup

3. . . . to drink?
(a cup of) coffee

4. . . . for breakfast?
(an order of) pancakes

5. . . . to drink?
(a glass of) red wine

6. . . . for dessert?
(a dish of) vanilla ice cream

7. . . . to drink?
(a cup of) hot chocolate

8. . . . for dessert?
(a bowl of) strawberries

9.

STANLEY'S FAVORITE RECIPES

Are you going to have a party soon? Do you want to cook something special? Stanley the chef recommends this recipe for VEGETABLE STEW. This is Stanley's favorite recipe for vegetable stew, and everybody says it's fantastic!

1. Put **a little butter** into a saucepan.

2. Chop up **a few onions.**

3. Cut up **(a little/a few)** _____

4. Pour in _____

5. Slice _____

6. Add _____

7. Chop up _____

8. Slice _____

9. Add _____

10. Cook for 3 hours.

When is your English teacher's birthday? Do you want to bake a special cake? Stanley the chef recommends this recipe for FRUITCAKE. This is Stanley's favorite recipe for fruitcake, and everybody says it's out of this world!

1. Put 3 cups of flour into a mixing bowl.

2. Add **a little sugar.**

3. Slice **(a little/a few)** _____

4. Cut up _____

5. Pour in _____

6. Add _____

7. Chop up _____

8. Add _____

9. Mix in _____

10. Bake for 45 minutes.

ON YOUR OWN

Do you have a favorite recipe?
Share it with other students in your class.

Future Tense: Will
Prepositions of Time
Might

```
I     will   I'll
He    will   He'll
She   will   She'll
It    will → It'll    } work.
We    will   We'll
You   will   You'll
They  will   They'll
```

```
Will he work?
Yes, he will.
```

A. Will the train arrive soon?

B. Yes, it will. It'll arrive in five minutes.

1. Will the soup be ready soon?
_____ in a few minutes.

2. Will Miss Blake be back soon?
_____ in an hour.

3. Will David finish school soon?
_____ in a month.

4. Will the tomatoes be ripe soon?
_____ in a few weeks.

5. Will Dr. Smith be here soon?
_____ in half an hour.

6. Will you get married soon?
_____ in a few months.

7. Will you be ready soon?
_____ in a few seconds.

8. Will the concert begin soon?
_____ at seven o'clock.

9. Will Mrs. Green be home soon?
_____ in a little while.

10. Will the flowers bloom soon?
_____ in April.

11. Will Betty get out of the hospital soon?
_____ in a few days.

12. Will Frank get out of jail soon?
_____ in a few months.

I He She It We You They	will work.

I He She It We You They	won't (will not) work.

WHAT DO YOU THINK?

Do you think it'll rain tomorrow?

Maybe **it** will, and maybe **it** won't. We'll just have to wait and see.

1. Do you think Cynthia will marry Norman?

2. Do you think it'll be very cold this winter?

3. Do you think you'll be happy in your new neighborhood?

4. Do you think Mary's husband will find a new job?

5. Do you think I'll be famous some day?

6. Do you think they'll have a baby soon?

7. Do you think there will be many people at the beach tomorrow?

8. Do you think we'll have to fight in a war some day?

9. Do you think _____?

125

I		
He		
She		
It	} might move to New York.
We		
You		
They		

A. When are you going to move to New York?

B. I don't know.
I might move to New York in a few weeks,
or I might move to New York in a few months.
I really can't decide.

A. Where are you going to go for your vacation?

B. We don't know.
We might go to Mexico, or we might go to Japan.
We really can't decide.

1. What kind of food is he going to cook tonight?

2. What color is she going to paint her kitchen?

3. When are you going to clean your apartment?

4. What are they going to name their new daughter?

5. What are they going to do tonight?

6. When are you two going to get married?

7. What are you going to buy your brother for his birthday?

8. What is he going to name his new puppy?

9. How are you going to come to class tomorrow?

10. What are you going to be when you grow up?

THE OPTIMIST AND THE PESSIMIST

A. Would you like to **go swimming** with me?

B. No, I don't think so.

A. Why not?

B. I'm afraid I might **drown.**

A. Don't worry! You won't **drown.**

B. Are you sure?

A. Yes, I'm positive!

B. O.K. I'll **go swimming** with you.

1. *go skiing*
break my leg

2. *go to a fancy restaurant*
get sick

3. *sit in the sun*
get a sunburn

4. *go dancing*
step on your feet

5. *take a walk in the park*
catch a cold

6. *go to Jack's party*
have a terrible time

7. *go sailing*
get seasick

8. *take a ride in the country*
get carsick

9. *share a bottle of wine*
get drunk

10. *go to the movies*
fall asleep

11. *go to a lecture*
be bored

12.

ON YOUR OWN

Be a pessimist! Using <u>might</u>, <u>might not</u>, <u>will</u>, <u>won't</u>, answer these questions.

1. Why don't you want to go to a party tonight?
2. Why don't you want to have dinner at a fancy restaurant?
3. Why don't you want to go to the movies tonight?
4. Why don't you want to buy a new car?

Comparatives
Should
Possessive Pronouns

| cold – colder | large – larger | big – bigger | easy – easier |
| short – shorter | safe – safer | hot – hotter | busy – busier |

A. I think you'll like my new apartment.

B. But I liked your OLD apartment. It was **large.**

A. That's right. But my new apartment is **larger.**

1. *bicycle*
fast

2. *refrigerator*
big

3. *car*
shiny

4. *dog*
friendly

5. *neighborhood*
safe

6. *living room rug*
soft

7. *sports car*
fancy

8. *recipe for vegetable stew*
easy

9. *wig*
pretty

cold	–	colder	
large	–	larger	
big	–	bigger	
easy	–	easier	

interesting	–	more interesting
intelligent	–	more intelligent
comfortable	–	more comfortable
beautiful	–	more beautiful

A. I think you'll like my new rocking chair.

B. But I liked your OLD rocking chair. It was **comfortable.**

A. That's right. But my new rocking chair is **more comfortable.**

1. *girlfriend
intelligent*

2. *boyfriend
handsome*

3. *watch
accurate*

4. *kitchen sink
large*

5. *house
beautiful*

6. *sofa
attractive*

7. *English teacher
smart*

8. *roommate
interesting*

9. *boss
nice*

10. *tennis racket
light*

11. *recipe for fruitcake
delicious*

12.

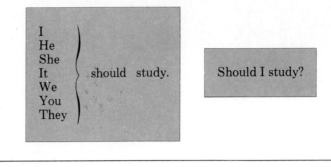

| I / He / She / It / We / You / They | should study. |

Should I study?

A. Should I buy a bicycle or a motorcycle?

B. I think you should buy a bicycle.

A. Why?*

B. Bicycles are **safer than** motorcycles.

A. Should he study English or Latin?

B. I think he should study English.

A. Why?*

B. English is **more useful than** Latin.

---

*Or: Why do you say that? What makes you say that? How come?

1. Should I buy a dog or a cat?

2. Should he buy a used car or a new car?

3. Should I vote for John Black or Peter Smith?

4. Should he go out on a date with Doris or Jane?

5. Should she go out on a date with Roger or Bill?

6. Should they buy a black-and-white TV or a color TV?

7. Should we buy this fan or that fan?

8. Should she buy these earrings or those earrings?

9. Should I plant flowers or vegetables this spring?

10. Should he study the piano with Mrs. Wong or Miss Schultz?

11. Should I buy the hat in my left hand or the hat in my right hand?

12. Should they go to the cafeteria up the street or the cafeteria down the street?

13. Should she buy fur gloves or leather gloves?

14. Should I go to the laundromat across the street or the laundromat around the corner?

15. Should I hire Miss Jones or Miss Wilson?

16. Should I fire Mr. Jackson or Mr. Brown?

17.

my	–	mine	our	–	ours
his	–	his	your	–	yours
her	–	hers	their	–	theirs

A. I'm jealous!
My dog isn't as friendly as your dog.

B. Don't be ridiculous!
Yours is MUCH friendlier than **mine.**

A. I'm jealous!
My novels aren't as interesting as Ernest Hemingway's novels.

B. Don't be ridiculous!
Yours are MUCH more interesting than **his.**

fast

1. *my car*
your car

comfortable

2. *my furniture*
your furniture

long

3. *my hair*
Rita's hair

nice

4. *my boss*
your boss

intelligent

5. *my children*
your children

big

6. *my house*
the Jones's house

clean

7. *my apartment*
your apartment

good-better

8. *my pronunciation*
Maria's pronunciation

delicious

9. *my recipe for fruitcake*
Stanley's recipe for fruitcake

popular

10. *my songs*
the Beatles' songs

important

11. *my job*
the President's job

12.

ON YOUR OWN

Read and practice.

In my opinion, New York is more interesting than San Francisco.

I disagree. I think San Francisco is MUCH more interesting than New York.

Do you think the weather in Miami is better than the weather in Honolulu?

No, I don't think so. I think the weather in Honolulu is MUCH better than the weather in Miami.

Are the people in Centerville as friendly as the people in Greenville?

No, the people in Centerville aren't as friendly as the people in Greenville, but they're more interesting. Do you agree?

Yes, I agree.

_____ er than
more _____ than

as _____ as
not as _____ as

Talk with other students about two cities: your home town and the city you live in now, or any two cities you know. Talk about . . .

the streets: quiet, safe, clean, wide, busy . . . ?
the buildings: high, modern, pretty . . . ?
the weather: cold, warm, rainy, snowy . . . ?
the people: friendly, nice, polite, honest, busy, happy, hospitable,
        talkative, healthy, wealthy, poor . . .?
the city in general: large, interesting, lively, exciting, expensive . . . ?

In your conversation you might want to use some of these expressions:

I agree.
I disagree.
I agree/disagree with (you, him, her, John . . .).

I think so.
I don't think so.
In my opinion, . . .

Superlatives

kind – the kindest		nice – the nicest	
cold – the coldest		safe – the safest	
busy – the busiest		big – the biggest	
happy – the happiest		hot – the hottest	

A. I think your friend Margaret is very **nice.**

B. She certainly is. She's **the nicest** person I know.

1. I think your cousin is very **friendly.**

2. I think your Uncle George is very **funny.**

3. I think your parents are very **kind.**

4. I think your older brother is very **shy.**

5. I think your cousin Nancy is very **pretty.**

6. I think Larry is very **lazy.**

7. I think the students in our class are very **smart.**

8. I think your Aunt Gertrude is very **cold.**

9. I think your younger brother is very **sloppy.**

kind	– the kindest	talented	– the most talented
busy	– the busiest	energetic	– the most energetic
nice	– the nicest	interesting	– the most interesting
big	– the biggest	polite	– the most polite

A. I think your grandmother is very **energetic.**

B. She certainly is.
She's **the most energetic** person I know.

1. I think your son is very **polite.**

2. I think John is very **stubborn.**

3. I think our English teacher is very **patient.**

4. I think your younger sister is very **talented.**

5. I think your older sister is very **bright.**

6. I think your upstairs neighbor is very **noisy.**

7. I think your downstairs neighbor is very **boring.**

8. I think your twin brothers are very **nice.**

9. I think your grandfather is very **generous.**

10. I think Walter is very **stingy.**

11. I think your girlfriend is very **honest.**

12.

a cheap typewriter	a comfortable chair	a good car
a cheaper typewriter	a more comfortable chair	a better car
the cheapest typewriter	the most comfortable chair	the best car

Read and practice.

IN THE DEPARTMENT STORE

A. May I help you?

B. Yes, please. I want to buy a **cheap** typewriter.

A. I think you'll like this one. It's VERY **cheap.**

B. Don't you have a **cheaper** typewriter?

A. No, I'm afraid not.
This is **the cheapest** one we have.

B. Thank you anyway.

A. Sorry we can't help you. Please come again.

A. May I help you?

B. Yes, please. I want to buy a/an _____ _____.

A. I think you'll like this one. It's VERY _____.

B. Don't you have a/an { _____er } _____?
   { more _____ }

A. No, I'm afraid not.
   This is the { _____est } one we have.
   { most_____ }

B. Thank you anyway.

A. Sorry we can't help you. Please come again.

1. *large refrigerator*

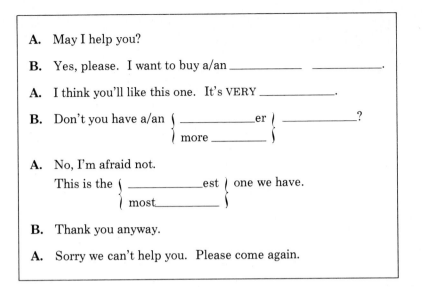

2. *comfortable rocking chair*

3. *good record player*

4. *fancy necktie*

5. *cheap watch*

6. *small kitchen table*

7. *good tape recorder*

8. *light tennis racket*

9. *elegant evening gown*

10. *modern sofa*

11. *short novel*

12.

good	bad
better	worse
best	worst

Answer these questions and then ask another student in your class. Give reasons for your opinions.

In your opinion . . .

1. Who is the most popular actor/actress in your country?

2. Who is the most popular TV star?

3. Who is the best singer? (What kind of songs does he/she sing?)

4. Who are the wealthiest people in your country? (What do they do for a living? Where do they live?)

5. Who is the most important person in your country now? (What does he/she do?)

6. Who is the most important person in the history of your country? (What did he/she do?)

In your opinion . . .

7. What is the best city in your country? Why?

8. What is the worst city in your country? Why?

9. What are the most interesting tourist sights for visitors to your country? (museums, monuments, churches . . .)

10. What are the most popular vacation places for people in your country? Why?

In your opinion . . .

11. What is the most popular car in your country?

12. What is the most popular sport?

13. What is the funniest TV program?

14. What is the best newspaper?

15. What is the most popular magazine?

16. What is the most popular food? (Do you know how to make it? If you know an easy recipe, share it with the students in your class.)

Directions

walk up
walk down
walk along

on the right
on the left

next to
across from
between

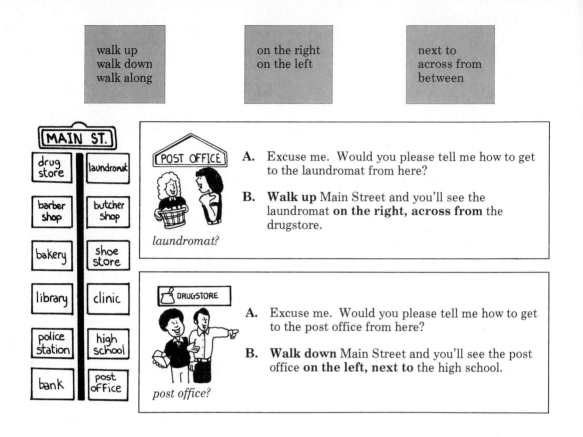

A. Excuse me. Would you please tell me how to get to the laundromat from here?

B. **Walk up** Main Street and you'll see the laundromat **on the right, across from** the drugstore.

laundromat?

A. Excuse me. Would you please tell me how to get to the post office from here?

B. **Walk down** Main Street and you'll see the post office **on the left, next to** the high school.

post office?

1. *shoe store?*

2. *police station?*

3. *high school?*

4. *barber shop?*

5. *butcher shop?*

6. *bank?*

144

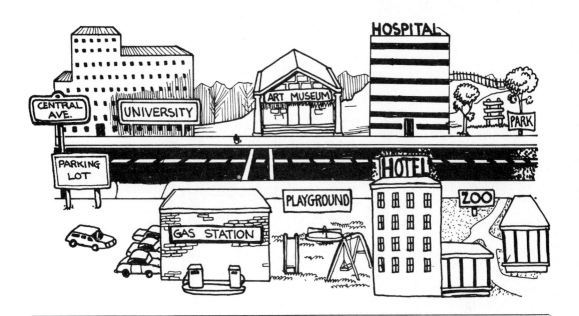

hospital?

A. Excuse me. Would you please tell me how to get to the hospital from here?

B. **Walk along** Central Avenue and you'll see the hospital **on the left, between** the art museum and the park.

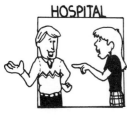

1. *parking lot?*

2. *university?*

3. *park?*

4. *art museum?*

5. *playground?*

6. *zoo?*

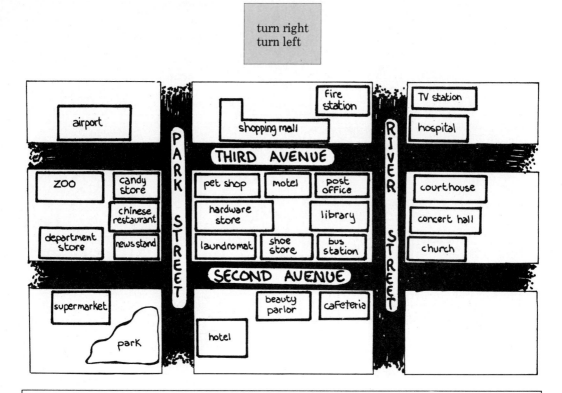

A. Excuse me. Would you please tell me how to get to the bus station from here?

B. **Walk up** Park Street to Second Avenue and **turn right.** **Walk along** Second Avenue and you'll see the bus station **on the left, across from** the cafeteria.

bus station?

A. Excuse me. Would you please tell me how to get to the concert hall from here?

B. **Drive along** Second Avenue to River Street and **turn left.** **Drive up** River Street and you'll see the concert hall **on the right, between** the courthouse and the church.

concert hall?

1. *shopping mall?*

2. *hardware store?*

3. *library?*

4. *zoo?*

5. *department store?*

6. *TV station?*

7. *hospital?*

8.

Take the bus and **get off** at Main Street.

A. Excuse me. What's the quickest way to get to Peter's Pet Shop?

B. **Take** the Main Street Bus and **get off** at First Avenue.
Walk up First Avenue and you'll see Peter's Pet Shop **on the right.**

A. Thank you for your help.

B. You're welcome.

A. Excuse me. What's the easiest way to get to Harry's Barber Shop?

B. **Take** the subway and **get off** at Fourth Avenue.
Walk down Fourth Avenue and you'll see Harry's Barber Shop **on the left.**

A. Thank you for your help.

B. You're welcome.

1. What's the fastest way to get to the baseball stadium?

2. What's the best way to get to St. Andrew's Church?

3. What's the most direct way to get to the zoo?

4. I'm in a hurry! What's the shortest way to get to the train station?

Read and practice.

GETTING AROUND TOWN

A. Can you recommend **a good hotel**?

B. Yes. The Bellview is **a good hotel**.
I think it's **one of the best hotels** in town.

A. Can you tell me how to get there?

B. Sure. Take the subway and get off at Brighton Boulevard. You'll see The Bellview at the corner of Brighton Boulevard and Twelfth Street.

A. Thank you very much.

B. You're welcome.

These people are visiting your city. Using the above conversation as a guide, help these people "get around town." Recommend real places you know and like, and give directions. If you disagree with another student's recommendation, explain why and recommend another place.

1. *a good restaurant?*

2. *a cheap department store?*

3. *a quiet, romantic cafe?*

4.

Adverbs
Comparative of Adverbs
Agent Nouns
If-Clauses

slow – slowly bad – badly beautiful – beautifully	terrible – terribly miserable – miserably simple – simply	sloppy – sloppily busy – busily lazy – lazily	fast – fast hard – hard good – well

work – a worker
play – a player
drive – a driver

A. I think he's **a careless driver.**

B. I agree. He **drives VERY carelessly**.

1. *a careless skier*

2. *a slow chess player*

3. *a beautiful singer*

4. *sloppy painters*

5. *an accurate translator*

6. *a good teacher*

7. *careful workers*

8. *a graceful dancer*

9. *good tennis players*

10. *dishonest card players*

11. *a fast driver*

12. *a hard worker*

softly – { softer / more softly }	carefully – more carefully
loud(ly) – { louder / more loudly }	politely – more politely
slowly – { slower / more slowly }	hard – harder
	fast – faster
neatly – { neater / more neatly }	early – earlier
	late – later

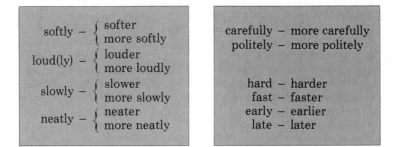

A. Bob speaks VERY **quickly**.

B. You're right. He should try to speak { **slower** / **more slowly** }.

1. Linda speaks very softly.

2. Ronald goes to bed very late.

3. Janet skates very carelessly.

4. Your friends come to class very early.

5. David types very slowly.

6. They dress very sloppily.

7. Peter speaks to his parents very impolitely.

8. Karen plays her record player very loud(ly).

9. They work very slowly.

What are they going to name their new baby?

If they have a boy, they'll name him John.
If they have a girl, they'll name her Jane.

1. How are you going to get to school tomorrow?

If it rains, I'll _____.
If it's sunny, I'll _____.

2. What's Bob going to do this Saturday afternoon?

If the weather is good, he'll _____.
If the weather is bad, he'll _____.

3. What's Carmen going to have for dinner tonight?

If she's very hungry, _____.
If she isn't very hungry, _____.

4. What's Fred going to do tomorrow?

If he feels better, _____.
If he doesn't feel better, _____.

5. When are you going to go to sleep tonight?

If I'm tired, _____.
If I'm not tired, _____.

6. What are they going to wear tomorrow?

If it's hot, _____.
If it's cool, _____.

Answer these questions and ask another student in your class.

1. What are you going to do tonight if you have a lot of homework?
2. What are you going to do tonight if you DON'T have a lot of homework?
3. What are you going to have for breakfast tomorrow if you're very hungry?
4. What are you going to have for breakfast tomorrow if you AREN'T very hungry?
5. What are you going to do this weekend if the weather is nice?
6. What are you going to do this weekend if the weather is bad?

EVERYBODY GIVES ME ADVICE

A. Everybody tells me I shouldn't drive **so fast**.

B. They're right.
If you drive **too fast**, you might **have an accident**.

1. My boss tells me I shouldn't work so slowly.
lose your job

2. My music teacher says I shouldn't sing so loud.
get a sore throat

3. My friends tell me I shouldn't worry so much.
get an ulcer

4. My dentist says I shouldn't eat so much candy.
get a toothache

5. My teacher told me I shouldn't do my homework so carelessly.
make too many mistakes

6. Our baby-sitter says we shouldn't go to bed so late.
be tired in the morning

7. My parents tell me I shouldn't watch so many scary TV programs.
have nightmares

8. Everybody tells me I shouldn't

_____.

They're right. If _____.

Read and practice.

SUPERSTITIONS

Many people believe that you'll have GOOD luck

if you find a four-leaf clover.
if you find a horseshoe.
if you give a new pair of shoes to a poor person.

You'll have BAD luck

if a black cat walks in front of you.
if you walk under a ladder.
if you open an umbrella in your house.
if you put your shoes on a table.
if you light three cigarettes with one match.

Here are some other superstitions.

If your right eye itches, you'll laugh soon.
If your left eye itches, you'll cry soon.

If your right ear itches, somebody is saying good things about you.
If your left ear itches, somebody is saying bad things about you.

If a knife falls, a man will visit soon.
If a fork falls, a woman will visit soon.
If a spoon falls, a baby or a fool will visit soon.

If you break a mirror, you'll have bad luck for seven years.

If you spill salt, you should throw a little salt over your left shoulder.
If you don't, you'll have bad luck.

Do you know any superstitions?
Share them with other students in your class.

Act this out in class.

PLEASE DON'T ASK ME A DIFFICULT QUESTION!

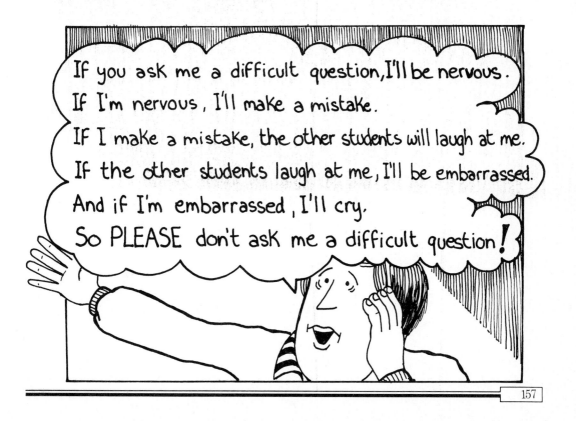

Past Continuous Tense
Reflexive Pronouns
While-Clauses

I He She It	was	working.
We You They	were	

THE BLACKOUT

Last night at 8:00 there was a blackout in Centerville. The lights went out all over town.

A. What was Doris doing last night when the lights went out?

B. She was taking a bath.

A. What were Mr. and Mrs. Green doing last night when the lights went out?

B. They were riding in an elevator.

Ask about these people.

1. *Ted*

2. *Irene*

3. *Bob and Judy*

4. *you*

5. *Joe*

6. *your parents*

7. *your younger sister*

8. *your father*

9. *Mr. and Mrs. Jones*

What were YOU doing last night at 8:00? Tell the other students in your class.

A. I saw you yesterday, but you didn't see me.

B. Really? When?

A. At about 2:30.
You were **getting out of a taxi on Main Street**.

B. That wasn't me.
Yesterday at 2:30 I was **cooking dinner**.

A. I guess I made a mistake.

1. *walking into the post office*
fixing my car

2. *walking out of the laundromat*
cleaning my apartment

3. *getting on a bus*
watching TV

4. *getting off a merry-go-round*
playing baseball

5. *jogging through the park*
playing tennis

6. *riding your bicycle along Main St.*
cooking

7. *getting out of a police car*
sleeping

8.

I	myself
you	yourself
he	himself
she	herself
it	itself
we	ourselves
you	yourselves
they	themselves

A. What did **John** do yesterday?

B. He went to the movies.

A. Who did he go to the movies with?

B. Nobody. He went to the movies **by himself**.

1. *Patty*
go to the beach

2. *Peter*
go to the ballgame

3. *you*
go bowling

4. *you and your wife*
play cards

5. *Mr. and Mrs. Jones*
have a picnic

6. *Mrs. Wilson*
drive to New York

7. *you*
go to Bob's party

8. *Mr. Wilson*
take a walk in the park

9.

A. You look upset.

B. Yes. I had a bad day today.

A. Why? What happened?

B. I **lost my wallet** while I was **jogging through the park.**

A. I'm sorry to hear that.*

A. Harry looks upset.

B. Yes. He had a bad day today.

A. Why? What happened?

B. He **cut himself** while he was **shaving**.

A. That's too bad.*

*Or: How awful! That's terrible! What a shame! What a pity!

1. *you*
burned myself
cooking dinner

2. *Sheila*
dropped her packages
walking out of the supermarket

3. *Tom*
hurt himself
playing basketball

4. *your parents*
got a flat tire
driving over a bridge

5. *you*
fainted
waiting for the bus

6. *Nelson*
saw a few gray hairs
looking at himself in the mirror

7. *you and your wife*
had an accident
driving home

8. *Linda*
cut herself
slicing a tomato

9. *you*
a dog bit me
standing on the corner

10. *Marvin*
tripped and fell
walking to work

11. *your aunt and uncle*
somebody stole their car
shopping

12. *you*
a can of paint fell on me
walking under a ladder

ON YOUR OWN

Everybody has a bad day once in a while. Try to remember a few days when something bad happened to you. What happened? And what were you doing when it happened? Share your sad stories with the other students in your class.

Could
Be Able to
Have Got to
Too + Adjective

I He She It We You They	can/can't	could/couldn't	study.

Could he study? Yes, he could. No, he couldn't.

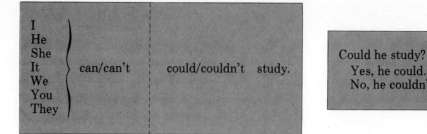

A. Could Peter play on the basketball team when he was a little boy?

B. No, he couldn't.
He was **too short**.

1. Could Henry go to work yesterday?
sick

2. Could Rita go out with her boyfriend last weekend?
busy

3. Could Mr. and Mrs. Jones finish their dinner?
full

4. Could Billy buy a drink at the bar last Saturday night?
young

5. Could you finish your homework last night?
tired

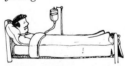

6. Could Frank get out of bed the day after his operation?
weak

7. Could Betty tell the policeman about her accident?
upset

8. Could Stuart eat at his wedding?
nervous

$$
\text{could} = \left\{ \begin{array}{l} \text{was} \\ \text{were} \end{array} \right\} \text{able to}
$$

$$
\text{couldn't} = \left\{ \begin{array}{l} \text{wasn't} \\ \text{weren't} \end{array} \right\} \text{able to}
$$

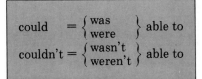

A. Was Jimmy able to lift his grandmother's suitcase?

B. No, he wasn't able to. It was **too heavy.**

1. Was Louise able to paint her house yesterday afternoon?
windy

2. Was Carl able to sit down on the bus this morning?
crowded

3. Were Mr. and Mrs. Johnson able to go swimming in the ocean during their vacation?
cold

4. Was Shirley able to finish her order of spaghetti and meatballs?
spicy

5. Was Tom able to find his wallet last night?
dark

6. Were you able to do the grammar exercises last night?
difficult

7. Could Jeff and Gloria see the full moon last night?
cloudy

8. Was Willy able to wear his brother's suit to the dance last Saturday night?
small

A. Did Barbara enjoy herself at the concert last night?

B. Unfortunately, she { wasn't able to / couldn't } go to the concert last night. She had to **study for an examination**.

1. Did Ronald enjoy himself at the baseball game yesterday?
go to the dentist

2. Did you enjoy yourself at the tennis match last week?
visit my boss in the hospital

3. Did Mr. and Mrs. Wilson enjoy themselves at the symphony yesterday evening?
wait for the plumber

4. Did Sally enjoy herself at the theater last Saturday night?
take care of her little brother

5. Did you enjoy yourself at the discotheque last night?
finish my homework

6. Did Fred enjoy himself at Mary's party last Friday evening?
work late at the office

7. Did you and your classmates enjoy yourselves at the movies last night?
study English

8. Did Marion enjoy herself at the picnic last Sunday?
take care of her neighbor's dog

9. Did you enjoy yourself at the football game yesterday?
fix a flat tire

10.

I've (I have) We've (we have) You've (you have) They've (they have)	} got to =	I We You They	} have to	
He's (he has) She's (she has) It's (it has)	} got to =	He She It	} has to	work.

Read and practice.

A. I'm afraid I won't be able to help you **move to your new apartment** tomorrow.

B. You won't? Why not?

A. I've got to **take my son to the doctor.**

B. Don't worry about it!
I'm sure I'll be able to **move to my new apartment** by myself.

A. I'm afraid I won't be able to help you _____ tomorrow.

B. You won't? Why not?

A. I've got to _____.

B. Don't worry about it!
I'm sure I'll be able to _____ by myself.

1. *clean your garage*
go to the bank

2. *paint your living room*
fly to Chicago

3. *fix your car*
drive my husband to the clinic

4. *do your homework*
practice the piano

5. *repair your kitchen window*
take care of my neighbor's baby

6. *cook Christmas dinner*
buy presents for my children

7. *study for the examination*
take my daughter to her ballet lesson

8. *take Jennifer to the dentist*
work late at the office

9. *take Rover to the vet*
visit my mother in the hospital

10.

Read and practice.

1.

George is upset.
He got a flat tire and he won't be able to get to the airport on time.

2.

Rita is frustrated.
She lost her key and she can't get into her apartment.

3.

Mrs. Brown's English class is really upset.
Mrs. Brown is sick and she won't be able to teach them English this week.

4.

Sidney is disappointed.
He wasn't able to find a job in New York City and he had to move home with his mother and father.

5.

Ted was really disappointed last year.
He couldn't dance in the school play.
His teacher said he was too clumsy.

Are you frustrated, disappointed, or upset about something? Tell the class about your problem. If you don't have a problem now, tell the class about the LAST time you were frustrated, disappointed, or upset.

Must
Must vs. Should
Fewer/Less
Past Tense Review

I		
He		
She		
It	} must work.
We		
You		
They		

more/less	more/fewer
bread	cookies
fish	potatoes
fruit	eggs

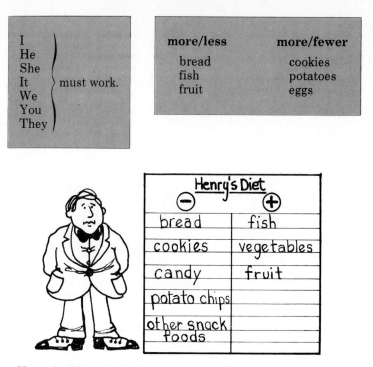

Henry's Diet	
⊖	⊕
bread	fish
cookies	vegetables
candy	fruit
potato chips	
other snack foods	

1. Henry had his yearly checkup today. The doctor told him he's a little too heavy and gave him this diet:

He must eat **less** bread, **fewer** cookies, **less** candy, and **fewer** potato chips and other snack foods.

Also, he must eat **more** fish, **more** vegetables, and **more** fruit.

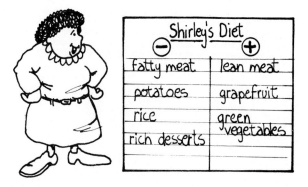

Shirley's Diet	
⊖	⊕
fatty meat	lean meat
potatoes	grapefruit
rice	green vegetables
rich desserts	

2. Shirley also had her annual checkup today. Her doctor gave her this diet:

She must eat _____

_____

_____

Arthur's Diet	
⊖	⊕
butter	margarine
eggs	skim milk
cheese	yogurt
ice cream	

3. Arthur was worried about his heart. He went to his doctor for an examination and the doctor told him to eat fewer fatty foods.

He must eat/drink _____

_____

_____

Rover's Diet	
⊖	⊕
fatty meat	lean meat
dog biscuits	water

4. Rover went to the vet yesterday for his yearly checkup. The vet told him he's a little too heavy and gave him this diet:

He must eat/drink _____

_____

_____

MY DIET	
⊖	⊕

5. You went to the doctor today for your annual physical examination. The doctor told you you're a little overweight and said you must go on a diet.

I must eat/drink _____

_____

_____

must/mustn't (must not)

A. I had my yearly checkup today.

B. What did the doctor say?

A. He/She told me I'm a little too heavy and I must lose some weight.

B. Do you have to stop eating _____?

A. No, I don't have to stop eating _____, but I mustn't eat as (much/many) _____ as I did before.

1.

2.

3.

4.

5.

6.

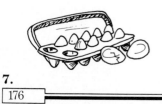

7.

8.

9.

THE CHECKUP

Read and practice.

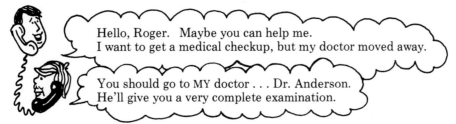

Hello, Roger. Maybe you can help me.
I want to get a medical checkup, but my doctor moved away.

You should go to MY doctor . . . Dr. Anderson.
He'll give you a very complete examination.

1.  The nurse will lead you into one of the examination rooms.

2.  You'll take off your clothes and put on a hospital gown.

3.  Dr. Anderson will come in, shake your hand, and say "hello."

4.  You'll stand on his scale so he can measure your height and your weight.

5.  He'll take your pulse.

6.  Then he'll take your blood pressure.

7. After he takes your blood pressure, he'll take some blood for a blood analysis.

8. He'll examine your eyes, ears, nose, and throat.

9. He'll listen to your heart with a stethoscope.

10. Then he'll take a chest X-ray and do a cardiogram (EKG).

YOUR CHECKUP

You had a complete physical
examination yesterday. Tell us about
your visit to the doctor.

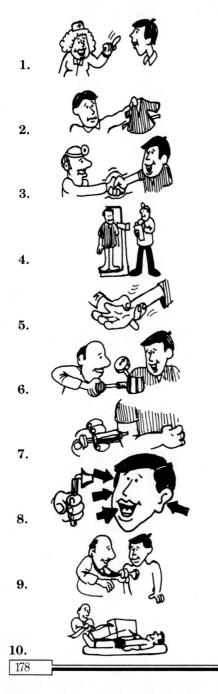

1.   The nurse **led** me _____.

2.   _____.

3.   _____.

4.   _____.

5.   _____.

6.   _____.

7.   _____.

8.   _____.

9.   _____.

10.   _____.

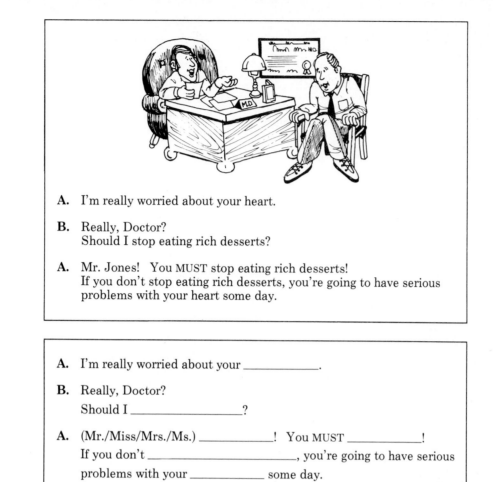

A. I'm really worried about your heart.

B. Really, Doctor?
Should I stop eating rich desserts?

A. Mr. Jones! You MUST stop eating rich desserts!
If you don't stop eating rich desserts, you're going to have serious
problems with your heart some day.

A. I'm really worried about your _____.

B. Really, Doctor?
Should I _____?

A. (Mr./Miss/Mrs./Ms.) _____! You MUST _____!
If you don't _____, you're going to have serious
problems with your _____ some day.

---

1. *lungs*
stop smoking

2. *liver*
stop drinking liquor

3. *blood pressure*
take life a little easier

4. *back*
start doing exercises

5. *ears*
*stop listening to loud
rock music*

6.

HOME REMEDIES

What do YOU do when you burn your finger?

Some people rub butter on their finger.

Other people put a piece of ice on their finger.

Other people put their finger under cold water.

Different people have different remedies for medical problems that aren't very serious. The people below need your advice. Help them with their medical problems and share your "home remedies" with the other students in your class.

1. I have a cold. What should I do?

2. I have a stomachache. What should I do?

3. I have a toothache. What should I do?

4. I have a bloody nose. What should I do?

5. I have the hiccups. What should I do?

Future Continuous Tense

I	will	I'll
He	will	He'll
She	will	She'll
It	will →	It'll
We	will	We'll
You	will	You'll
They	will	They'll

} be working.

A. Will you be home this evening?
B. Yes, I will. I'll be reading.

1. *Sharon*

2. *Steven*

3. *Mr. and Mrs. Williams*

4. *Bob*

5. *you*

6. *Kathy*

7. *Jack*

8. *you*

9. *Mrs. McDonald*

10. *you and your brother*

11. *Dave*

12. *you*

Read and practice.

A. Hi, Gloria. This is Arthur. Can I come over and visit this evening?

B. No, Arthur. I'm afraid I won't be home this evening. I'll be shopping at the supermarket.

A. Can I come over and visit TOMORROW evening?

B. No, Arthur. I'm afraid I won't be home tomorrow evening. I'll be working late at the office.

A. Can I come over and visit this WEEKEND?

B. No, Arthur. I'll be visiting my sister in New York.

A. Can I come over and visit next Wednesday?

B. No, Arthur. I'll be visiting my uncle in the hospital.

A. How about some time next SPRING?

B. No, Arthur. I'll be getting married next spring.

A. Oh!

B. Good-bye.

Complete this conversation.

I'm having some problems with the homework for tomorrow.

I'll be glad to help.
When can you come over?

I can come over at _____ o'clock.
Is that O.K.?

I'm afraid I won't be home at _____ o'clock.
I'll be _____ing. How about _____ o'clock?

No, I won't be able to come over at _____ o'clock.
I'll be _____ing. How about _____ o'clock?

Fine. I'll see you then.

A. How long will your Aunt Gertrude be staying with us?

B. She'll be staying with us **for a few months.**

1. How long will they be staying in San Francisco?
until Friday

2. How much longer will you be working on my car?
for a few more hours

3. How late will your husband be working tonight?
until 10 o'clock

4. Where will you be getting off?
at the last stop

5. How much longer will you be practicing the piano?
for a few more minutes

6. How late will your daughter be studying English this evening?
until 8 o'clock

7. When will we be arriving in London?
at 7 a.m.

8. How much longer will you be reading?
until I finish this chapter

9. How far will we be driving today?
until we reach Detroit

10. How soon will Santa Claus be coming?
in a few days

Read and practice.

A. Hello, Richard.   This is Julie.
I want to return the tennis racket I borrowed from you last week.
Will you be home today at about five o'clock?

B. Yes, I will.   I'll be cooking dinner.

A. Oh, well.   Then I won't come over at five.

B. Why not?

A. I don't want to disturb you.   You'll be cooking dinner!

B. Don't worry.   You won't disturb me.

A. O.K.   I'll see you at five.

A. Hello, _____. This is _____.
I want to return the _____ I borrowed from you last week.
Will you be home today at about _____ o'clock?

B. Yes, I will. I'll be _____ing.

A. Oh, well. Then I won't come over at _____.

B. Why not?

A. I don't want to disturb you. You'll be _____ing!

B. Don't worry. You won't disturb me.

A. O.K. I'll see you at _____.

1. *book*
   doing the laundry

2. *record*
   watching my favorite TV program

3. *hammer*
   helping my son with his homework

4. *coffee pot*
   knitting

5. *football*
   ironing

6.

Some/Any
Pronoun Review
Verb Tense Review

I	me	my	mine	myself
you	you	your	yours	yourself
he	him	his	his	himself
she	her	her	hers	herself
it	it	its	its	itself
we	us	our	ours	ourselves
you	you	your	yours	yourselves
they	them	their	theirs	themselves

A. What's **Johnny** doing?

B. **He's** getting dressed.

A. Does **he** need any help?
I'll be glad to help **him**.

B. No, that's O.K.
He can get dressed by **himself**.

1. *your husband*
fix the TV

2. *your daughter*
feed the canary

3. *your children*
cook breakfast

4. *you and your husband*
clean the garage

5. *your sister*
fix her car

6. *your son*
take out the garbage

7. *Bobby and Billy*
clean their bedroom

8. *you*
do my homework

9.

A. I just found this watch. Is it yours?

B. No, it isn't mine. But it might be **Fred's**.
He lost **his** a few days ago.

A. Thanks. I'll call **him** right away.

1. *umbrella*
Susan's

2. *briefcase*
John's

3. *pocketbook*
Maria's

4. *wallet*
George's

5. *camera*
Mr. and Mrs. Green's

6. *notebook*
Margaret's

7. *ring*
Albert's

8. *transistor radio*
Bobby and Billy's

9. *address book*
Edward's

10. *sneakers*
Helen's

11. *glasses*
Elizabeth's

12.

A. You look tired today.

B. Yes, I know. I couldn't fall asleep last night.

A. Why not?

B. My **neighbors** were **arguing**.

A. How late did they **argue**?

B. They **argued** until 3 a.m.

A. That's terrible! Did you call and complain?

B. No, I didn't. I don't like to complain.

A. Well, I hope you sleep better tonight.

B. I'm sure I will. My **neighbors** don't **argue** very often.

1. *neighbor's son
practice the violin*

2. *neighbor's dog
bark*

3. *neighbor's daughter*
listen to her stereo

4. *upstairs neighbors*
play cards

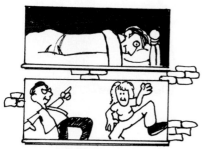

5. *downstairs neighbors*
dance

6. *neighbor across the hall*
sing

7. *next door neighbors*
clean their apartment

8. *neighbor's daughter*
play the piano

9. *neighbor's son*
lift weights

10.

something	anything
somebody someone	anybody anyone

A. There's something wrong with my **washing machine**.

B. I'm sorry. I can't help you.
I don't know ANYTHING about **washing machines**.

A. Do you know anybody who can help me?

B. Not really. You should look in the phone book.*
I'm sure you'll find somebody who can fix your **washing machine**.

*You can also say, "in the yellow pages." Businesses are listed in the yellow pages of the telephone book.

1. *stove*

4. *kitchen sink*

7. *piano*

2. *TV*

5. *bathtub*

8. *radiator*

3. *refrigerator*

6. *dishwasher*

9.

Read and practice this conversation.

A. Hello. May I please speak to Mr. Armstrong?

B. This is Mr. Armstrong. Can I help you?

A. Yes. There's something wrong with my kitchen sink and I need a good plumber who can come over and fix it as soon as possible.

B. Where do you live?

A. I live at 156 Grove Street in Centerville.

B. I can come over tomorrow at four o'clock. Is that O.K.?

A. Not really. I'm afraid I won't be home tomorrow at four o'clock. I'll be taking my son to the dentist. Can you come at any other time?

B. Not this week. I'm really busy.
I won't be able to come over until some time next week.

A. That's too late. I guess I'll have to call somebody else.
Thank you anyway.

B. Good-bye.

A. Good-bye.

A. Hello. May I please speak to (Mr./Mrs./Miss/Ms.) _____?

B. This is (Mr./Mrs./Miss/Ms.) _____. Can I help you?

A. Yes. There's something wrong with my _____ and I need a good _____ who can come over and fix it as soon as possible.

B. Where do you live?

A. I live at _____ in _____.

B. I can come over tomorrow at _____ o'clock. Is that O.K.?

A. Not really. I'm afraid I won't be home tomorrow at _____ o'clock. I'll be _____ing. Can you come at any other time?

B. Not this week. I'm really busy. I won't be able to come over until some time next week.

A. That's too late. I guess I'll have to call somebody else. Thank you anyway.

B. Good-bye.

A. Good-bye.

1. *electrician*

2. *TV repairman*

3. *piano tuner*

4. *plumber*

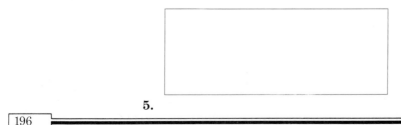

5.

APPENDIX

**Cardinal Numbers
Ordinal Numbers
Irregular Verbs:
Past Tense**

Cardinal Numbers

1	one	13	thirteen	20	twenty
2	two	14	fourteen	21	twenty-one
3	three	15	fifteen	22	twenty-two
4	four	16	sixteen	.	.
5	five	17	seventeen	.	.
6	six	18	eighteen	29	twenty-nine
7	seven	19	nineteen	30	thirty
8	eight			40	forty
9	nine			50	fifty
10	ten			60	sixty
11	eleven			70	seventy
12	twelve			80	eighty
				90	ninety

100	one hundred	1,000	one thousand
200	two hundred	2,000	two thousand
300	three hundred	3,000	three thousand
.	.	.	.
.	.	.	.
.	.	10,000	ten thousand
900	nine hundred	100,000	one hundred thousand
		1,000,000	one million

Ordinal Numbers

1st	first	13th	thirteenth	20th	twentieth
2nd	second	14th	fourteenth	21st	twenty-first
3rd	third	15th	fifteenth	22nd	twenty-second
4th	fourth	16th	sixteenth	.	.
5th	fifth	17th	seventeenth	.	.
6th	sixth	18th	eighteenth	29th	twenty-ninth
7th	seventh	19th	nineteenth	30th	thirtieth
8th	eighth			40th	fortieth
9th	ninth			50th	fiftieth
10th	tenth			60th	sixtieth
11th	eleventh			70th	seventieth
12th	twelfth			80th	eightieth
				90th	ninetieth

one hundredth

one thousandth

one millionth

How to read a date:

June 9, 1941 = "June ninth, nineteen forty-one"

Irregular Verbs: Past Tense

be	was	light	lit
begin	began	lose	lost
bite	bit	make	made
break	broke	meet	met
bring	brought	put	put
buy	bought	read	read
catch	caught	ride	rode
come	came	run	ran
cut	cut	say	said
do	did	see	saw
drink	drank	sell	sold
drive	drove	send	sent
eat	ate	shake	shook
fall	fell	sing	sang
feed	fed	sit	sat
feel	felt	sleep	slept
fight	fought	speak	spoke
find	found	stand	stood
fly	flew	steal	stole
forget	forgot	sweep	swept
get	got	swim	swam
give	gave	take	took
go	went	teach	taught
grow	grew	tell	told
have	had	think	thought
hear	heard	throw	threw
hurt	hurt	understand	understood
know	knew	wear	wore
lead	led	write	wrote
leave	left		

Index

Word List

The number after each word indicates the page where the word first appears.

(adj) = adjective,   (adv) = adverb,   (n) = noun,   (v) = verb

This word list does not include words that first appeared in Book 1A.

A

able to   167
accident   155
accurate   131
add   121
address book   191
advice   155
a few   115
afraid   127
after   166
again   109
ago   108
airport   146
a little   115
a little while   124
all over town   160
along   144
a lot   119
analysis   177
anybody   194
anyone   194
anything   109
apple   112
argue/arguing   192
arrive   124
art museum   145
as   135
at the corner   149
attractive   131
avenue   146
awful   163

B

baby-sitter   155
back (adv)   124
back (n)   179
bad   115
badly   153
bag   118
bake   113
baking soda   121
ballet   170
banana   112
bar   166
bark   192
baseball stadium   148
basketball   163
bean(s)   112

beautifully   153
beer   112
believe   156
best   140
better   134
bigger   130
birthday   108
bit   164
black-and-white TV   132
blackout   160
blood   177
blood pressure   177
bloody nose   180
bloom   124
bored   128
boring   139
borrow(ed)   186
bottle   118
bowl   120
box   118
boy   154
boyfriend   108
break   127
bridge   163
bright   139
bunch   118
burn(ed)   163
busier   130
busily   152
business(es)   194
butter   112

C

café   149
cake   113
can (n)   118
canary   190
candy   108
cardiogram   177
card player   152
care   115
careful   152
carefully   153
careless   152
carrot   118
carsick   128
catch a cold   127
certainly   138
chair   140

chapter   185
checkup   174
cheese   112
chess player   152
chicken   113
chicken soup   120
chocolate   120
chocolate cake   115
chop up   121
classmate(s)   168
clover   156
clumsy   171
coffee pot   187
colder   130
color TV   132
come   126
come over   183
complain   192
complete   177
concert hall   146
convenient   133
cookie   112
corner   149
cost   119
could   166
country   128
courthouse   146
cracker   112
crowded   167
cup   120
cut up   121

D

dance (n)   167
dark   167
decide   120
delicious   115
dessert   107
diet   174
direct   148
disagree   135
disappointed   171
dish   120
dishonest   152
disturb   186
dog biscuit (s)   175
do (ing) the laundry   187
doll   108
dollar   119

永和店：永和路 2 段224號　☎：504-1020
大直店：大直街 6 2 巷 2 號　☎：621-6066
淡水店：淡水鎮英專路 4 號　☎：422-8645
中壢一店：中壢市建國路62號　☎：425-4651
中壢二店：中壢市新生路57號　☎：229-8278
台中店：中市三民路三段117-4號